Wisdom from
RICH DAD POOR DAD FOR TEENS

THE SECRETS ABOUT MONEY—
THAT YOU DON'T LEARN IN SCHOOL!

ROBERT T. KIYOSAKI

RUNNING PRESS
PHILADELPHIA · LONDON

A Running Press® Miniature Edition™
Abridgement © 2009, 2016

This Little Book has been adapted from *Rich Dad Poor Dad for Teens* published by Plata Publishing.

Copyright © 2004, 2011 by Robert T. Kiyosaki.

All rights reserved under the Pan-American and International Copyright Conventions

Printed in China

This book may not be reproduced in whole or in part, in any form or by any means, electronic or mechanical, including photocopying, recording, or by any information storage and retrieval system now known or hereafter invented, without written permission from the publisher.

The proprietary trade dress, including the size and format, of this Running Press® Miniature Edition™ is the property of Running Press. It may not be used or reproduced without the express written permission of Running Press.

9 8 7 6 5 4 3 2 1
Digit on the right indicates the number of this printing

Library of Congress Control Number: 2016945242

ISBN 978-0-7624-6100-4

Published by Running Press Book Publishers,
An Imprint of Perseus Books, a Division of PBG Publishing, LLC,
A Subsidiary of Hachette Book Group, Inc.
2300 Chestnut Street
Philadelphia, PA 19103-4371

Visit us on the web!
www.runningpress.com

Contents

INTRODUCTION
Your Journey to Financial
Freedom Begins Here . . . 6

CHAPTER ONE
Financial Intelligence:
A New Way of Learning . . . 14

CHAPTER TWO
Rich Dad's Money Secret:
The New Rules
for Making Money . . . 28

CHAPTER THREE
Rich Dad's Money Secret: Work to Learn, Not to Earn . . . 38

CHAPTER FOUR
Rich Dad's Money Secret: "My Money Works for Me" . . . 52

CHAPTER FIVE
Rich Dad's Money Secret: Create Money . . . 60

CHAPTER SIX
Rich Dad's Money Secret: It's All About Cash Flow . . . 70

CHAPTER SEVEN
Rich Dad's Money Secret: Play Games to Learn . . . 84

CHAPTER EIGHT
Moneymaking Opportunities for Teens . . . 92

CHAPTER NINE
Managing Your Assets . . . 108

CHAPTER TEN
Managing Your Debt . . . 120

Conclusion   127

INTRODUCTION

Your Journey to Financial Freedom Begins Here

Take This Quiz:

Do you feel that school's not really preparing you for the real world?

    yes   no
    ☐   ☐

When you want to buy something that's important to you, do your parents usually say they can't afford it?

    yes   no
    ☐   ☐

Do you secretly worry that you won't be able to live the way you want when you're out on your own?

        yes   no
        ☐   ☐

Do you really want to learn about money, but no one talks about it around your house or at school?

        yes   no
        ☐   ☐

If you answered "yes" to two or more of these questions, this book is for you.

Financial Literacy

Congratulations for picking up this book! *Wisdom from Rich Dad Poor Dad for Teens* will teach you one of the most important subjects that isn't being taught in school: financial literacy. This book will give you the language and understanding you need to feel confident about taking charge of your financial life, whether that means starting your own business or just being able to hold your own in a conversation with someone who might become your financial mentor—your own "Rich Dad."

By the time you finish this book, you'll be able to speak the language of money more fluently. Your journey to financial literacy starts right here, right now.

Thinking in Numbers

Adults often view money as a "necessary evil"—something needed to pay bills, to count and recount, to obsess and worry about. But like it or not, money is something that will always be in your life, so you need to be comfortable with it—not afraid of it, like so many adults are. If you're educated about how money works, you gain power over it and can begin building wealth

School Is Just the Beginning

Unless you're planning to become a doctor or lawyer or go into a profession that requires a special degree, you may not need to go to any formal training programs after high school or college to earn money if you look for great learning opportunities in a job.

Am I saying that education isn't important? Not at all. Education is the foundation of success. I'm saying that school is just one place to learn. We go to school to learn academic and professional skills. For the most part, we learn financial skills out in the world. Amazing, isn't it, to think that you might be getting knowledge that your parents might not have?

CHAPTER ONE

Financial Intelligence: A New Way of Learning

You Are Smart

First of all, let's get one thing straight: You are smart! When I was growing up, my dad always told me that everyone is born smart—that every child has a special kind of genius.

But we all learn differently. The trick is to find the way you learn best. When you do that, you'll discover your own personal genius.

What's Your Learning Style?

Take a look at this list. As you read it, think about what methods best describe your learning style. Circle the number that matches up for each of the learning styles: 1 is least like you and 5 is most like you.

This is not a test! There's no right or wrong answer or high or low score. This is just a way to think about how you learn most comfortably.

Verbal-linguistic intelligence

If you always have a book tucked in your backpack, circle 5.

1	2	3	4	5

Numerical intelligence

If you're one of those people who can do a math problem in your head, circle 5.

1	2	3	4	5

Spatial intelligence

If doodling helps you listen in class, or if you're always seeing things that you'd like to photograph, circle 5.

1 2 3 4 5

Musical intelligence

Are you tapping a pencil or drumming your fingers right now? Head for the number 5.

1 2 3 4 5

Physical intelligence

If you love PE in school, or if your room looks like a sporting-goods store, circle 5.

1   2   3   **4**   5

Interpersonal intelligence

Do friendships seem effortless to you (mark 5) or endlessly complicated (mark 1)?

1   2   3   *4*   5

Intrapersonal intelligence

If you are self-aware, or good at handling your emotions in stressful situations, circle 5.

1   2   3   *4*   5

Natural Intelligence

If you are sensitive to the world around you and enjoy the outdoors or working for the environment, circle 5.

1   2   3   4   5

Vision

If you can see how a situation will play out and take action in response, mark 5.

1   2   3   4   5

Do you notice a pattern to your numbers? Where did you rank yourself highest?

If you are:

- High ranking in verbal-linguistic: You are comfortable with reading and writing as tools for learning.

- High ranking in physical, musical, or natural intelligences: You may have great success in "learning by doing"—using on-the-job training such as internships or being involved in school and community clubs.

- High ranking in spatial or numerical

intelligences: You may benefit from learning through drawing, making charts and diagrams, building models, or working with your hands.

- High ranking in interpersonal or verbal-linguistic intelligences or vision: You may learn best by talking with friends or grown-ups about their experiences, by debating, or by performing.

It's also possible that you ranked yourself high in several areas. That means that you'll be comfortable with "mixing and matching" different activities that work with your learning styles.

But what if you didn't rank yourself high in any area? Are you doomed? Not at all. This exercise was designed to help you start to think about how you think. If you're stronger in one area than others, there's a lot you can do to balance out.

Here are some suggestions.

- Talk about money at home and with your friends. (Verbal-linguistic and interpersonal intelligences)

- Read about it! Lots of magazines about money and finance show how money works in real life, rather than in textbook math problems. (Verbal-linguistic and numerical intelligences)

- Write about it! Use a journal to explore ideas about the role money plays in your life now and in the future. (Intrapersonal and verbal-linguistic intelligences and vision)

- If you get an allowance, take it seriously. Figure out ways to earn it and invest it. (Numerical and interpersonal intelligences)

- Do your own audit. Once a week, do an accounting of where your money has gone. (Numerical intelligence)

- Decide to become responsible for your future. Create a positive attitude about money. (Intrapersonal intelligence and vision)

Develop Your Financial IQ

The road to a high financial IQ is to work on your money skills using the intelligences that work for you—and work to develop the others so that your whole brain is working full-steam. Try a few different learning styles on for size. It might not be until the second or third try that you feel you're working with the right combination.

Believe It

The best way to get what you want is to believe you can get it. Thoughts are powerful. Turning a thought around can create a mindset that will make something happen. That intention teamed with the financial education you'll get from this book is a powerful combination.

CHAPTER TWO

Rich Dad's Money Secret: The New Rules for Making Money

The Old Rules Don't Apply Anymore

What if I told you that having a profession is not the only way to earn money—especially if you want to make a lot of money? Having a job will certainly earn you a living, but working for a salary isn't the most effective path. This path will probably lead you right into the Rat Race—where you work to earn, work harder to earn more, and eventually burn out.

The Rich Think Differently

My dad was Superintendent of Education for the State of Hawaii. Though my father was well respected, he didn't make lots of money.

Because of where my family lived,

I went to the same public school as the rich kids. By being in school with kids who were rich, I could see that they had a different outlook about money. Parents of my friends seemed so confident about the future. They actually thought differently about money, I realized.

I also knew that the rich kids learned things at home that I wasn't learning in my house. They learned to have a confident attitude about money.

From my earliest childhood, I

decided I wanted to be rich. I decided I liked the idea of having money and all the nice things it could buy. I also liked the idea that rich parents wouldn't have to worry about paying bills and supporting their kids as much as my dad did.

What You Think Is What You Get

In school, my best friend Mike and I spent lots of time together, and we hung out after school, too. In a way, we even shared each other's dad!

My dad and Mike's dad were very different. I would sum up their difference this way: My dad said, "The love of money is the root of all evil." Mike's dad said, "The lack of money is the root of all evil."

My two dads' very different views on money taught me that "what you think is what you get!"

"The reason I'm not rich
is because I have you kids."

"When it comes to money,
don't take risks."

"Work for benefits."

"Save."

"The reason I must be rich is because I have you kids."

"Learn to manage risks."

"Be totally self-reliant financially."

"Invest."

The Haves and the Have-Nots

People sometimes talk about the "haves" and the "have-nots," and that the "haves"—the rich—think differently.

If you work in a job with a specific salary, then chances are you're not going to have much vision beyond your paycheck. But let's say you're thinking like a rich person. Your work is to discover ways to make extra money without working longer hours, ways to start your own business. Your work is to discover new possibilities. Sounds exciting, right?

CHAPTER THREE

Rich Dad's Money Secret: Work to Learn, Not to Earn

My First Job

Mike's dad worked for the sugar plantation, but he also owned warehouses, a construction company, a chain of stores (superettes), and three restaurants. He offered us a job at one of the superettes for 10 cents an hour.

"You work for me," he said, "and I'll teach you, but I won't do it classroom-style. I can teach you faster if you work, and I'm wasting my time if you just want to sit and listen, like you do in school. That's my offer. Take it or leave it."

Mike's dad was talking about a whole new kind of learning. We took the job.

Mike and I reported to Mrs. Martin, who ran one of the stores that Mike's dad owned. She put us to work dusting and re-stacking canned goods in her store. It was one of the most boring things I've ever done.

Mike and I hated every minute of

our job. After three weeks of working on the weekends, I was completely fed up and ready to quit. I felt angry, cheated, and exploited. We were doing all this work for just ten cents an hour! Even in 1956, that wasn't much money at all. I decided I had to do something about it. I was going to talk to Mike's dad.

Standing Up to My Boss

The next Saturday, I went to Mike's house at eight o'clock in the morning. "Take a seat and wait in line," Mike's dad told me, and disappeared into his little office next to a bedroom. So I waited in the living room with other people who worked for Mike's dad who also wanted to have a meeting with him . . . and waited . . . and waited.

Eventually, I was the only person left, and still rich dad didn't come out of his office to call me in to speak with him.

When rich dad finally signaled for me to come in, I was angrier than I had ever felt in my life. "You promised to teach me and you aren't holding up your end of the bargain," I accused. I was standing up to a grown-up and it felt good, but scary at the same time.

Instead of being angry with me, rich dad seemed pleased that I'd spoken up. "So," he asked, "Does *teaching* to you mean talking, or a lecture?"

"Yes," I answered.

"That's how they teach you in school," he said with a smile. "But that's not how life teaches you, and I would say that life is the best teacher of all. It just sort of pushes you around. Each push is life saying, 'Wake up and learn.'" Rich dad said that when life pushed me around, I needed to push back. By going to rich dad to tell him my problems with the job, I had learned to push back.

Is "pushing back" always the right thing to do?

Not always. Even though rich dad taught me to "push back," he also taught me not to let my emotions—especially fear—make my decisions for me. Here are some examples of things you might say when emotions are doing the thinking and making the choices.

What You're Saying:
My friend is always talking to me in class, so I can't do my best work.

What You're Saying:
I don't have a trust fund like my rich friend. I don't see the point in trying to become rich if I have nothing to start with, like she does.

What You're Thinking:
It's his fault, not mine.

What You Fear:
I don't have control over this situation.

What You're Thinking:
I resent my friend because she has financial security and I don't.

What You Fear:
The odds are against me.

When a situation "pushes your buttons," take a step back and try to assess the situation coolly, using your inter- and intrapersonal intelligences. These skills will also help you in the business world when working with difficult people.

What Did Your First Job Teach You?

What It Means to Work

Rich dad told me, "Money is an illusion." He told me to imagine a donkey dragging a cart with its owner dangling a carrot in front, moving the carrot further forward with every step the donkey takes. The donkey is chasing an illusion.

This is true with working, rich dad explained. The carrot is like a toy. The toys we want get bigger and bigger and more expensive as we get older.

So what's the solution? People who are already rich seem to know it: Work to learn and to have your money work for you. Rich dad wanted me to find the power to create money rather than to work for money. "If you do not need money," rich dad said, "you will make a lot of money."

Create Your Own "Think Tank"

When you do repetitive tasks as part of a job or chore, it may seem like counting sheep at bedtime—boring enough to put you to sleep! But the truth is that it actually provides an opportunity for quiet time that can free your mind to do some creative thinking . . . and creative thinking is key in Rich Dad's secrets for success!

CHAPTER FOUR

Rich Dad's Money Secret: "My Money Works for Me"

Life Is Filled with Surprises

I may have been just a kid, but I'd survived a tough business meeting with rich dad. I had stood up to him and he had seemed to be saying it was okay. Amazing! Rich dad patted me on the back and suggested I get back to work. The next thing he said to me caught me by surprise. "This time, I will pay you nothing." I was supposed to "work to learn, not to earn." Somehow, I had to believe that dusting and stacking cans would teach me something, because I wasn't going to get a single penny for my time.

Rich dad said, "Keep working, boys, but the sooner you forget about needing a paycheck, the easier your life will be when you are adults. Keep using your brain, work for free, and soon your mind will show you ways of making money far beyond what I could ever pay you. Most people never see opportunities because they're looking for money and security, so that's all they get. The moment you see one opportunity, you will start seeing opportunities for the rest of your life."

A Comic Twist

One day, a few weeks later, I noticed Mrs. Martin cutting the front page of a comic book in half and throwing the rest of it into a large brown cardboard box. I asked her what she was doing, and she told me that she was going to get credit for the unsold comic books. The distributor needed to see only the part of the front page she was returning. The rest of the comic book was no good to her or to the distributor.

But it could be a gold mine for Mike and me.

We talked to the distributor the next time he came into the store. "You can have these comics if you work for this store and do not resell them," he told us. A light bulb went on in my head. Mike and I were soon in business with a moneymaking plan.

A Surefire Business Opportunity

Here's how we figured it: A comic cost 10 cents each in those days. Most kids could read five or six comics in one sitting. That would come to sixty cents if they bought the comics. But if they came to a place where they could just read the comics without buying them, and if we charged them an admission fee, they would come out ahead—and so would we.

We charged 10 cents admission to any kid who wanted to come and read comics during two hours each weekday that our library was open. A lot of kids used our library. We averaged $9.50 per week over a three-month period. We were on our way to being rich.

CHAPTER FIVE

Rich Dad's Money Secret: Create Money

Where Does Income Come From?

Where does money come from? It sounds like a dumb question, but you'd be surprised by how many people don't know the complete answer to it.

Types of Income

There are three ways to earn money. Working at a job is one of the ways. But there are two other ways to make money that are actually more effective.

The three basic types of income are:

Earned income. Earned income is money you get from working. When you have a job, you're paid an hourly wage or salary—usually in a paycheck you get every week or every two weeks.

Passive income. Passive income is earned even when you're not physically doing any work. Passive income can come from businesses that you set up that someone else runs on a day-to-day basis.

Portfolio income. If you have money invested in paper assets (stocks, bonds, or mutual funds), you have portfolio income. Portfolio income works on the same principle as passive income.

What's the best kind of income?

Rich dad often told me, "The key to becoming rich will be your ability to convert earned income into passive income and portfolio income." He also told me that the taxes are highest on earned income and lowest on passive income.

The Only Thing You Need to Remember Is . . .

One day, when Mike and I were in rich dad's office, he told us that if we wanted to be rich, there was really only one thing we needed to remember: "Know the difference between assets and liabilities," he said, "and buy assets."

Assets = Put Money in Your Pocket

Rich dad's first definition, which I've never forgotten, was that an asset puts money into your pocket. An asset should generate income on a regular basis. While you might consider everything of value in your room an "asset" (like a computer or a TV, because you could sell it for decent money on eBay), it's not really an asset until it is sold. Why? Because it's not putting any money into your pocket until then.

Liabilities = Take Money Out of Your Pocket

Liabilities are the opposite of assets. Liabilities take money out of your pocket. Liabilities also include everything that you owe. If you borrow money from a friend, or from your sister or brother, the debt is a liability. If you pay for something with a credit card, creating debt, that's a liability as well. And, of course, the taxes you need to pay are a liability.

Asset or Liability?

Assets can be deceiving. Something that might seem like an asset can turn into a liability.

The solution, I'm happy to say, is an easy one that most people know about but often don't act on: Buy assets that produce income. What's a teenager to do, you might be asking?

Buy carefully. Don't overspend on doodads.

So . . .
- **Assets** put money in your pocket.

- **Liabilities** take money out of your pocket.

- Buy assets that produce income.

CHAPTER SIX

Rich Dad's Money Secret: It's All About Cash Flow

Financial Statements: Reading the Numbers

A financial statement shows the relationship between what you have and what you owe. It's made up of two parts: an income statement and a balance sheet.

An income statement shows what money is coming in and what money is going out and gives you an idea at a glance of what money you might have available.

A balance sheet shows the relationship between assets and liabilities.

The pattern of money coming in and going out is called cash flow.

The top half of the financial statement, the income and expense boxes, is your income statement. The bottom portion, the asset and liability boxes, is

Income

Expense

Assets	Liabilities

your balance sheet.

Ideally, we want more income than expenses, and more assets than liabilities.

The Cash Flow Pattern of an Asset

This is what the cash flow pattern of an asset looks like.

The arrow, representing the flow of money, is going from the assets box to the income box, meaning that the asset is generating money.

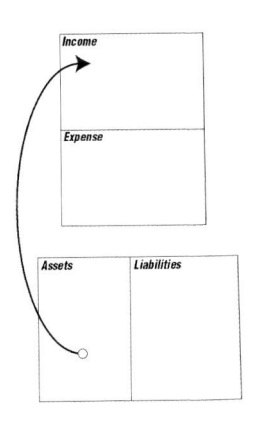

Income

Expense

Assets	Liabilities

The Cash Flow Pattern of a Liability

The cash flow pattern of a liability would look like this:

The cash flow **arrow** would go from the liabilities **section** to the expense section, and **then** it would go off the chart, meaning **that** the money is gone.

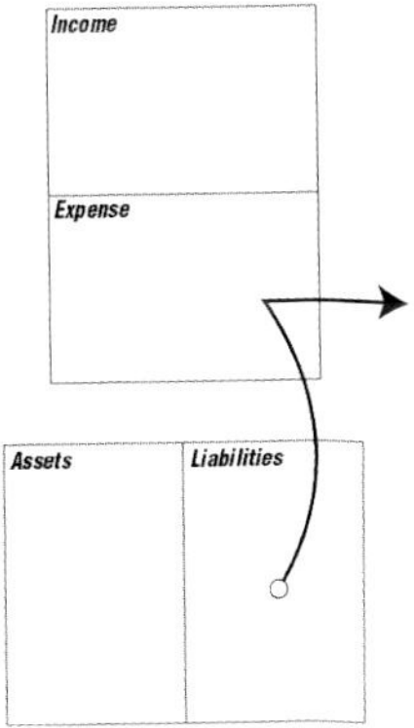

Income	
Expense	

Assets	*Liabilities*

Is it possible to have money and still be poor?

Yes. This seems like a contradiction, but it can happen.

The amount of earned income is not directly proportional to your total wealth. My dad had "a good job" that paid a decent salary, but he never broke his poor dad habits. Mike's dad might have earned almost the same (or even less) money than my dad from his job at the sugar plantation, but he invested it well and became rich.

If you keep as much in the asset box as you can and as little in the liability box as you can, you'll be rich. It's that simple. Instead of "I *have* to have that," you might start to think, "Do I have something similar at home?"

Where Are You Financially?

Now it's your turn! Using the same four boxes (labeled *Income, Expense, Asset, Liability*), you can easily create your own financial statement. Fill in your income and expenses, stocks, bonds, or bank accounts in your assets box, then list any liabilities you might have: a car loan or any debt you might owe. To get your net worth subtract the liabilities from the assets.

Where Does Your Money Go?

Here's an exercise: Keep track of what you spend for just one day. If you can find a tiny notebook, put it inside your wallet so that you'll see it when you need to pay for something. Every time you buy something, write it down. Using this method will increase your awareness of how often you reach for your wallet.

Stretching the Dollar

If you know what you spend your money on, you'll be able to make decisions about how to trim your spending. In addition, there are lots and lots of ways to stretch your dollar. Here are some examples.

- Think about ways to "recycle" old clothing.

- Instead of having lunch out all the

time with your friends, have lunch at someone's house.

- If there are any supplies that you buy on a regular basis buy them in bulk and buy them on sale.

CHAPTER SEVEN

Rich Dad's Money Secret: Play Games to Learn

Poor Dad: "Study to learn."

Rich Dad: "Play games to learn."

Play to Learn!

Rich dad used to say, "Games are a reflection of real life. The more you play, the richer you become." What a great concept—life represented by a game board. I loved it! I had always loved playing Monopoly®.

The game Monopoly is all about real estate on the surface, but it uses all of the principles about money, such as assets and passive income that I introduced in the last chapter.

From the Rat Race to the Fast Track

Ninety percent of the population lives in the Rat Race, always struggling to pay bills and living from paycheck to paycheck. They think that getting a raise is a solution to their problems, but getting more money usually means wanting and buying more liabilities, which leads them even deeper into the Rat Race, and deeper into debt.

In CASHFLOW®, the goal is to get your income from investments (your passive income) to be greater than your expenses so that you can go out and pursue your dreams rather than worry about working for your paycheck. Playing games like CASHFLOW is really good practice for life. It's a way for you to make use of all your learning styles, to strengthen your financial intelligence, and to think like a rich person. As your financial IQ gets higher, you'll be able to avoid the Rat Race in real life.

Field Trips

Another great learning opportunity is the field trip. These field trips are not so much physical excursions as they are fact-finding missions that allow you to "play along" in real-life situations.

Here are some examples:

- Ask your parents if you can sit with them while they pay their bills.

- Ask your parents if you can look at

their financial statement—or create one with them.

- Arrange to go to work with one of your parents or a friend's parent to get an idea of what a workday is like.

- If your parents are going to buy a car or major household appliance like a refrigerator or washing machine, go with them. Ask them to explain their decision to either pay cash or to finance the purchase in another way, and how it affects their monthly budget and financial statement.

All of these "field trips" will allow you to understand more about (and possibly participate in) the financial matters of your family and will help you become more financially responsible.

CHAPTER EIGHT

Moneymaking Opportunities for Teens

"I'm just a teenager without a trust fund. How do I get some cash flowing in?"

Work to Learn, Not to Earn

There are many ways to make money, even if you're 16 or younger. I guarantee that you—yes, you—can offer a skill or service that people want and need and are willing to pay for. Instead of being an employee, be an entrepreneur.

Work Is an Exchange

Rich dad told me, "You can have anything as long as you're willing to exchange something of value for what you want." The more I gave, the more I got in return.

In order to create a fair exchange, you must learn what each job is worth to you. You must look for opportunity, not salary. Working to learn means that you're usually getting back something much greater than the time you're giving up—in addition to the cash!

What if I want to work, but my parents won't let me?

Suppose you want to get an after-school job, but your parents simply say "no." Ask them why. If the reason is that they fear it will take time away from your school studies, you need to consider whether or not they might be right.

On the other hand, if you truly want to work to learn, and you can convince your parents of that, they may think again. Most parents will support their kids' desires—and efforts—to learn. When your parents see you being innovative and entrepreneurial, they're likely to begin to understand what your motivations and talents are. Chances are they do want to nurture and encourage those qualities in you!

Business Brainstorming

A lot of young people don't even realize that there's work that's available to them even in their early teen years.

Here's a list of jobs where you can be in business for yourself:

- Be a tutor.

- Teach people of all ages how to use the computer.

- Baby-sit for a younger neighbor.

- Water plants or walk dogs while neighbors are away.

- Be a personal assistant: Type letters, do research.

- Make personalized T-shirts.

What other ideas can you come up with?

FYI:
Things You Can't Do

Since different states have different laws, I strongly recommend that you check out the U.S. Department of Labor Web site (www.dol.gov) before starting a specific job. There you'll find a detailed listing of age-related rules for the entire country and for specific states.

Where to Look for Work

When you start looking for work, you can be on the lookout for an opportunity every waking moment.

Here are some places to look for work:
- Ask family, friends, neighbors, and parents of your friends. Ask everyone you know!

- Look on bulletin boards in your school, supermarkets near where you live, and the public library.

- Go to stores where you like to shop and ask if there are jobs available.

- Check out listings at your Chamber of Commerce.

- Ask at your place of worship, community clubs, and youth associations.

- Check the Internet.

- Check listings in the newspaper.

It's worth noting that as exciting as looking for work opportunities can be, you should be careful, too. Discuss your job search with your parents and keep them posted every step of the way. And remember, stay away from jobs in which you raise money for someone else.

A Few Things About Your Paycheck

The downside of working—even if you're working to learn—is that you'll be exposed to paying taxes for the first time. Fortunately, at your age, filing a tax return is usually fairly straightforward.

With each paycheck, a certain amount of money is also taken out and put away for your retirement, deductions for Social Security and Medicare. So remember that if you agree to work 10 hours a week for $5.00 an hour, you won't be taking home $50 in cash at week's end.

It's very difficult to make a lot of money if you rely solely on your paycheck. But at least your paycheck will help get your cash flow in motion.

Ask an Expert/ Find a Mentor

Rich dad was my mentor when I was growing up. The best way to find out about working is to find your own mentor—someone who's successful in the field you want to pursue.

Your mentor is like a one-on-one coach, someone you can turn to when you have questions. More rewarding, though, is the fact that you'll have discovered your own personal role model who inspires you. A mentor is someone who cares about you, too. He or she can check in with you on a regular basis and give you honest feedback on what you've done.

CHAPTER NINE
Managing Your Assets

The Piggy-Bank Approach

Okay, so now you're working, looking for a job, or maybe just thinking about earning money. When you make money, you're going to need to put it somewhere.

What I learned from rich dad is

that no matter what age you are, you should have a piggy bank—and not just one piggy bank. Rich dad recommended that I have three piggy banks, each one for a specific purpose.

Piggy Bank #1 = Charity

One of the really great things about being rich is the ability to help others. To be truly rich, we need to be able to give as well as receive. When it comes time to send money to a charity, tell your parents what you intend to do. As much as we like to think that everyone is honest, there are some scam artists out there who pretend to be raising money for charities but who are only helping themselves. Your parents can help you make sure that an organization is accredited.

When sending your contribution, it's best to send a check or money order. These are the safest way to send money through the mail and it's a good record of your contribution. Charitable contributions are tax deductible, which means that the more contributions you make, the less you pay in taxes.

Piggy Bank #2 = Savings

The idea is to have a backup of savings, money that is tucked away safely for a "rainy day." While it's important to have something in this piggy bank, it's also not important to put all of your leftover income after expenses into it.

Here's why: Most saving accounts pay you interest—that is, a percentage of the total in your account—each month. It's kind of a way of encouraging you to keep your money in the bank—so the bank can use it instead. But the truth of the matter is that the interest usually doesn't amount to much. The place where you'll see real results is putting money into your assets.

Piggy Bank #3 = Investments

My third piggy bank was for investments and represented risk and learning, and buying and building assets. As you now know, the third piggy bank is the one that rich dad taught me to focus on. The second piggy bank is the one that most people think they need to focus on. But since investments typically earn more money than savings accounts, rich dad knew that the third piggy bank deserved much more attention in order to create wealth.

Financial intelligence allows you to work or not work, to buy whatever you want without worrying about the price, or to give money away to a charity or cause that is important to you. Money without financial intelligence is money soon gone.

Grow Your Money

But what does it mean to "take care" of your money?

After learning about the three piggy banks, you might think it's all about sitting on your money. Filling those piggy banks is only a part of the formula. The other part of the formula is what may seem like exactly the opposite—it's about keeping your money moving.

Pay Yourself First

As soon as you've earned some money, the first place you should put your money is back into your piggy bank.

On the following page is the financial statement of a woman who has paid herself first. Each month she puts money into the asset (income) column before she pays her monthly expenses of her mortgage and her school tuition. Even when she's a little short of money, she pays herself

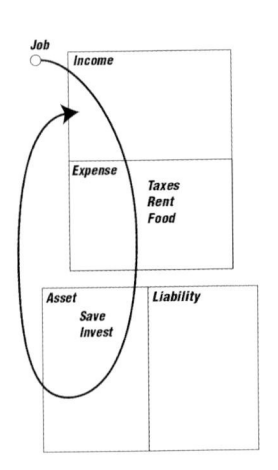

Job	Income
	Expense — Taxes, Rent, Food
Asset — Save, Invest	Liability

first. She does not dip into her savings, even when she comes up a little bit short once in a while, it really makes her think about how to make up the difference.

CHAPTER TEN

Managing Your Debt

Good Debt and Bad Debt

You're probably wondering how managing debt—instead of getting rid of debt—can be an important lesson in a book about getting rich.

My poor dad worked hard all his life to get out of debt.

Rich dad worked hard all his life to get into debt. "If you want to be rich," he would say, "you must know the difference between good debt and bad debt."

Credit Card Basics

If you can't resist temptations to buy doodads and have trouble keeping money in your wallet, having a credit card makes it even harder to hang on to your money.

With real money, you actually see the bills. With a credit card, all you take out is a piece of plastic and sign for it. That's it! The process is so easy, you hardly know you're paying for something. And that can be dangerous.

The Downward Spiral

Having a credit card can get you into trouble. With this magic piece of plastic, you can now buy things with money you don't have. Having a credit card is like having a blank check—until the bill comes. It's surprising how quickly your purchases make it to your billing statement. And here's where the trouble really starts.

The credit card statement has a date of when your payment is due the amount due and the minimum payment due. If you pay off your debt using the minimum payment option, chances are pretty high that whatever you bought will break or go out of style long before you pay for it.

Paying the minimum amount due on your balance usually means you'll have to pay the price of an extremely high interest rate. In case you didn't know, that's the percentage of your grand total owed that is *added* to your bill each month. So each month your bill grows without your even buying anything new. It's worse than spending money on a liability—it's almost as if you were flushing the money right down the toilet.

Take control of your credit card bills before they spin out of control. If you buy something on a credit card, make an effort to pay for it in full when the bill comes.

Credit cards can be your worst nightmare, but not always. In fact, if you use a credit card wisely—that is, if you pay your bill on time—you'll have an excellent opportunity to establish a good credit rating. That will help you later in life when you need to borrow money to buy assets that will bring you passive income. Credit cards also help you keep track of how you are spending your money.

Choose Wisely!

I have only one last bit of advice for you right now:

Choose your friends and mentors wisely. Be careful from whom you take advice. If you want to go somewhere, it's best to find someone who's already been there. Choose to spend time with people who understand and appreciate your vision and goals. Even better, choose people who share them!

This book has been bound using
handcraft methods and Smyth-sewn
to ensure durability.

The text was written by
Robert T. Kiyosaki.

The text was set in Garamond,
Helvetica, and Snell Roundhand.